BLISHING
eet #168
O 64030
Publishing.com

lene Melissa
PP Team Designers
hit Dey

hat Purpose Publishing has made the stylistic choice to
tain words and pronouns that refer to the Father, Son, and the
although it may differ from the stylistic choice of other

United States of America

BA
IN DA

Words Tha
Prayers That H

Brenda Hi

PURPOSE PU
1503 Main Str
Grandview, M
www.Purpose

Purpose
www.PurposeF

SPECIAL ACKNOWLEDGEMENTS

My mother, Jeffie Hicks, is my true inspiration. She made me who I am today. If it wasn't for the discipline, spankings, and sitting down eating dinner together my life probably would have taken a different route. But because of the Godly advice and a Godly woman praying her way through life, it kept me on the right road. The road was bumpy more times than many, but we kept pushing our way through. I love you, Mama.

I thank God for my husband, Twayne Wiggins. My rock, my boo, my sidekick, and my best friend. We have endured many trials and tribulations, but through the grace of God we've made it. Over the mountains and through the woods, we made it. You have been the best husband I could've ever ask for. It's been 31 years since we got married and I pray to God that we will celebrate even more years to come. When I am stressed, you are my peace. When you are stressed, I pray for you. I love that we pray together and seek God first, above all else. I love you!

My daughters are my world. Where would I be without them? You, three amazing girls, who have grown into beautiful masterpieces created by God, called women. You all have shown me so much in life. I wasn't the perfect mother, but I tried my best. When I couldn't guide you, God took you all by the hand and led you down the right paths and I'm grateful. Now look at yawl, all grown, up with children of your own. I thank God for each of you, my daughters, who are always there for mother. I love you girls!

My grandkids keep me young. I love you all of the same! I always tell people, I have a big baby and the little ones. You all are always in my heart. I pray to God daily to keep you all safe in His arm of protection and that He keeps His hand on your lives forever. You all just keep my laughing even when I don't feel like it. You keep me going! My grandkids are all beautiful gifts from God. I am extremely blessed. I love you grandkids!

Everyone that picked up this prayer book. I pray that you will enjoy it and laugh! I know that so many of you will be able to relate to the *"Back in Da' Day"* way of living. As well, to the younger generation who will also see this book too, I want you to realize that we were the *first* hip hop generation. We certainly had it going on back then. It may not seem like it to you, but when we were living it, we had a blast. But now, through you all, we can truly see how strong our parents, grandparents, aunts, uncles, and cousins all played an important part in our lives. We were family and we all helped keep us together. Thank you to everyone who is part of my life, now and then. And to all the new friends I'm making as you read this book. Welcome to my family and thank you for welcoming me into yours!

I pray that this book is a blessing to all who read it because it was truly a blessing to me to write it.

many of you will be able to relate to... and to...
Do you have any of these? As well as the larger
selection above I also see this person I want to...
formality that we were the ones helping rebecca...
We even only had it going to a later... it may not
seem like... to you, but what these were to me... we
had a blast. Surround through you all, we can talk
etc. how story... but parents, grandparents, aunts,
uncles, and cousins all pitched in to make... our
our first... We were family, and we all helped keep
us together. Thank you to everyone who is part of
my life, now and then. And to all the new friends
I'm making as you read this book. Welcome to my
family and thank you for welcoming me into yours.

I pray that this book has blessed you, as it has me
because it was truly a blessing to me to present.

Know your worth,
Embrace your worth,
And don't ever hide your worth
Brenda Hicks-Wiggins

CONTENTS

INTRODUCTION

Back in Da' Day is a book of prayers, some hilarious, but all are real. How did we survive in this world turned upside down? Coming from *Back in Da' Day*, we survived off of the prayers of our family - mama's, grandma's, grandpa's, uncle's, aunt's, Godparents, and so on. We made it through, some of us on a wing and a prayer.

These prayers are God given to me, straight from the heart of Our Father. One night, I found myself just talking to God about life and how to survive. That's right. I am an older woman *still* trying to survive today. It gets tough for me sometimes or should I say, more than many, times it's gotten tough. And I'd bet you could say the same thing for you too. But God! With God, I've taken a licking, but He keeps me ticking. He gave me the vision for this hilarious prayer book. It's prayers that every day people can relate to. You will find out that in this world, like mama said, *"Just keep on living"* that you'll have to laugh sometimes to keep from crying.

These are prayers that will heal your soul and fill your spirit with laughter. Laughter is like medicine to the soul. **Proverbs 17:22** NKJV tells us, *"A merry heart does good, like medicine, But a broken spirit dries the bones."* When I think about how my childhood was, I thank God. In my childhood, we could go outside, play, be kids and have fun. We had it all - life, laughter, and love.

The moral to these prayers (some hilarious) are to make you laugh in the midst of the trials and tribulations we face and go through on a daily basis. Whether they are big or small, old or young - we all go through. But God brings laughter into our lives to let us know, everything is going to be alright.

"And we know that all things work together for good to those who love God, to those who are the called according to His purpose." Romans 8:28 NKJV

FROM ONE GENERATION

Do you remember, *Back in Da' Day*, when times were good? Children were outside and playing. We played all kinds of games like: hopscotch, devil in the pitchfork, rubber band rope, hide and seek, little Sally Walker, Old Mary Mack, and so many more outside games. We had a curfew. It was to be inside or in front of the house when the street lights came on. And if you were not in your rightful place when mama or daddy came to the screen door, they would holler your name to come inside. OMG, wasn't that embarrassing! Then, you'd be on punishment for the next couple of days. We got whooping's. I mean, we got our butts spanked. And guess what? We had to go outside and pick your own switch. Do you remember that? And, if you went and got the wrong size switch, you were sent back outside to pick out another one. Mama and daddy, didn't play.

No they did not. They meant what they said and said what they meant.

We went to church every Sunday. Most of the time, it was several times on the same Sunday. We had Sunday school, regular service and another service in the evening. You didn't have a choice. You went and that was it; nothing else said. We had choir rehearsal, bible study, and vacation bible study in the summer. Those were the good old days. I know the new generations now look back at that and say, "that is so whack or so crazy". They just don't know about those things. This new breed only knows video games, cell phones, social media- Instagram and twitter. This generation has more gadgets than I can even think of now days. It's different, but *Back in Da' Day* life was alright with me.

In our teenage years, we went to sock-hops. It only cost 25 cents to get in. We had fun laughing, dancing, eating and acting like kids. We were just having fun. We went skating, to the bowling alley, and the Drive-In movies. We walked to the theaters. As a matter of fact, we walked everywhere. We didn't worry about driving. We had fun catching the bus or walking. Teens now days don't know what it is to catch the bus or walk for that matter.

What happened? Where did we go wrong? No, I'm trying to figure out why is there so much anger in the world today. Why children don't love their parents or don't obey their parents? They appears as though they don't have a care in the world. Many don't want to go to school to get an education. I've heard that some don't even want a career. And never think about getting married. They don't want to raise their children and some don't even want to have children. All they want to do is party, hangout, buy guns, kill people and think they can get away with it.

The generation that is supposed to take our place, when the time comes, is slowly fading away. The devil has come and whispered in the ear of this new generation. They've listened to the lies of the enemy and terrible things he speaks. The devil tries to make them think that everything they do is ok. The devil is a liar. He has no respect for people. He does not care for people. He is evil and angry. It's not acceptable and He cannot have our children or grandchildren.

This generation is crying out to us to help. I know sometimes we don't know how or don't want to get involved. But God put these prayers on my heart to pass on to the generation to come. So, I'm praying for a change of heart and a change of mind for all our young people, this new generation. I pray their hearts will be taken over by the Lord and He will help them see a bright, beautiful future for themselves and their families like we did Back in Da' Day. I want you to join me in these prayers.

PEACE

Lord,

Thank you for this day. Lord, help me to keep my tongue right today. Help me to not get upset over things that are out of my control. Don't let me fly off the handle today, slam a door, or throw something that should be kept on the ground. Father God, grant me your peace!

Amen!

Philippians 4:7 NKJV

"And the peace of God, which passeth all understanding, shall keep your hearts and minds through Christ Jesus."

Philippians 4:7 The Message Bible (MSG)

"Don't fret or worry. Instead of worrying, pray. Let petitions and praises shape your worries into prayers, letting God know your concerns. Before

you know it, a sense of God's wholeness, everything coming together for good, will come and settle you down. It's wonderful what happens when Christ displaces worry at the center of your life."

Back in Da' Day, I remember growing up and slamming the door, because I was mad at my mom. In response, I heard her say, "Don't let the doorknob hit you where the good Lord split you." That was enough to stop me from ever slamming doors again and flying off the handle. Moma gave me peace for rest of my life.

RESPECT

Lord Jesus,

Let us be thankful for the good old days and the days we are living in right now. Let us show respect, give respect; show love, give love and surely thank God for every single day. Forgive us for talking back, mumbling under our breath, and rolling our eyes when someone is talking to us. I am talking to the young and the old on that. This is something that we are all very familiar with and should not do. Help us to listen and learn instead of just thinking we know it all. Help us Lord, right now. In the Name of Jesus!

Amen!

Hebrews 12:11 New King James Version (NKJV)

"Now no chastening seems to be joyful for the present, but painful; nevertheless, afterward it yields

the peaceable fruit of righteousness to those who have been trained by it."

Hebrews 12:11 The Message (MSG)

"In this all-out match against sin, others have suffered far worse than you, to say nothing of what Jesus went through—all that bloodshed! So don't feel sorry for yourselves. Or have you forgotten how good parents treat children, and that God regards you as his children?

My dear child, don't shrug off God's discipline, but don't be crushed by it either. It's the child he loves that he disciplines; the child he embraces, he also corrects.

God is educating you; that's why you must never drop out. He's treating you as dear children. This trouble you're in isn't punishment; its training, the normal experience of children. Only irresponsible parents leave children to fend for themselves. Would you prefer an irresponsible God? We respect our own parents for training and not spoiling us, so why not embrace God's training so we can truly live? While we were children, our parents did what seemed best to them. But God is doing what is best for us, training us to live God's holy best. At the time, discipline isn't much fun. It always feels like it's going against the grain. Later, of course, it pays off handsomely, for it's the well-trained who find themselves mature in their relationship with God."

Back in Da' Day, I remember back in the day talking back to my mother and she told me "Girl I will slap you into to next week". I thought to myself, boy, your hand is going to hurt you because that is a long slap. But guess what? I didn't talk back. I wanted to enjoy the week. LOL!

OBEDIENCE

Jesus,

Cussing and fussing is the only way some people know how to speak and live. They can't say not one word without a cuss word coming out of their mouth. They are always fussing about this and that, seeming to enjoy it. Then, they wonder why and how the children are using those same bad words that they didn't think they'd know about. Not having anything good to say about anything. You see them coming and you turn the other way. You know the types, 'Negative Nancy' and 'Tuff Luck Tim'. God, we need help with our tongue. Help us Jesus. Amen.

The Bible says that life is in the power of the tongue. We can speak life with our tongues, or take away life with our tongues. How are you using yours?

Proverbs 18:21 New King James Version

"Death and life are in the power of the tongue and those who love it will eat its fruit."

Proverbs 18:21 The Message Bible (MSG)

"Words kill, words give life; they're either poison or fruit—you choose."

Back in Da' Day, My mother said to me once, "If I hear you say that one more time, I'm going to wash your mouth out with soap". I should have had the cleanest mouth. LOL! But the truth is, we need to watch what we say, how we say it, when we say it, and who we say it too. Words hurt. Words kill. There is no need of cussing. It will not change a thing. It only makes the matter worst, you've upset yourself because you have acted like a fool, cussing and fussing. Even after the other person is long gone, sitting at home with their feet propped up, smoking a cigarette, saying" Yep, I really upset them", next.

PROVIDER

Lord,

Thank you for the food on our table. Thank you for providing us with the funds to buy food for our families. Lord, show us not to waste food. Growing up we would always hear, "stop wasting food, there are people starving every day." And that's so true, there are literally millions of many people going hungry every single day in America and around the world. Show us how to help the next person in line and not be so greedy with our blessings. Help us to stop trying to keep everything for ourselves. Lord, show us how to take the leftovers and make them into something good.

Amen!

1 Timothy 5:8 New King James Version (NKJV)

"But if anyone does not provide for his own, and especially for those of his household, he has denied the faith and is worse than an unbeliever."

1 Timothy 5:8 The Message Bible (MSG)

"Take care of widows who are destitute. If a widow has family members to take care of her, let them learn that religion begins at their own doorstep and that they should pay back with gratitude some of what they have received. This pleases God immensely. You can tell a legitimate widow by the way she has put all her hope in God, praying to him constantly for the needs of others as well as her own. But a widow who exploits people's emotions and pocketbooks—well, there's nothing to her. Tell these things to the people so that they will do the right thing in their extended family. Anyone who neglects to care for family members in need repudiates the faith. That's worse than refusing to believe in the first place."

Back in Da' Day, we didn't waste food. We didn't get up from the table until our plate was clean. That's right. We ate leftovers all of the time. We didn't complain about the food that was cooked because if you did, you went to bed hungry. It was not considered abuse either.

Do you remember dropping a piece of candy or whatever you were eating at the time and it hit the ground. We'd say, "I kiss this up to God" or "God kiss it, devil miss it" – pick it back up, put it in our mouth and keep on playing. We ate it and didn't get sick.

APPRECIATE

Jesus,

Teach us how to appreciate the things that we have and stop longing for so much more. Sometimes it seems like we just beg you for stuff that we really don't need. The things that we do need, we don't ask. We crave materialistic things that really and truly have no value. We need to crave you Lord Jesus. We need to seek you Lord instead of the world. I know we all love to have nice things, but let's make sure that we that the nicest thing that life can give us and that is Jesus Christ.

Amen!

Matthew 6:33 New King James Version (NKJV)

"But seek first the kingdom of God and His righteousness, and all these things shall be added to you."

Matthew 6:33 The Message Bible (MSG)

"If God gives such attention to the appearance of wild-flowers—most of which are never even seen—don't you think he'll attend to you, take pride in you, and do his best for you? What I'm trying to do here is to get you to relax, to not be so preoccupied with getting, so you can respond to God's giving. People who don't know God and the way he works fuss over these things, but you know both God and how he works. Steep your life in God-reality, God-initiative, and God-provisions. Don't worry about missing out. You'll find all your everyday human concerns will be met."

Back in Da' Day, I was a teenager and my mother bought me a pair of gold earrings with my initials on them. She bought them from Famous Barr, a fine department store. (This was a long time ago). They were beautiful earrings, but I didn't want to wear them because I wanted to be like my friends. They all wore the cheap earrings that I thought looked good and hip. To this day, I think about those earrings and how much my mother sacrificed to buy them. They were gold earrings and she got them just for me. I wish I had those earrings today. This is a word for all, appreciate what you have and what you have been given. Just think, I chose a pair of earrings that tarnished in a few weeks over 14K gold which would've lasted a lifetime. What was I thinking? I guess I wasn't.

THANKFUL

Lord Jesus,

Let us be thankful for the good old days and even for the days we are living now. Let us show respect, give respect, show love, give love and make sure that we thank God for each day. Forgive us for talking back, mumbling under our breath. Please forgive us for rolling our eyes when someone is talking and we don't want to hear. This goes for the young and old. Ths is something that we can all learn from and do better. We act like we know it all and got it all together, but the truth is that we don't. Help us Lord right now, In the Name of Jesus!

Amen!

1 Thessalonians 5:18
New King James Version

In everything give thanks; for this is the will of God in Christ Jesus for you.

1 Thessalonians 5:18
The Message

16-18 Be cheerful no matter what; pray all the time; thank God no matter what happens. This is the way God wants you who belong to Christ Jesus to live.

Back in da day: I remember my moma saying to me that if you are not thankful or grateful for the things that I buy you, I will give them all to the someone who will appreciate them. Always keep and have a grateful attitude in life, that will take you far. Well, after that, I kept the words grateful, thankful in my mouth and had an attitude of gratitude.

REFUGE

Lord Jesus,

I know that family is very important. It is a beautiful time to sit down and break bread together. This is a rare thing now in household today. We don't eat together, pray together, talk, laugh, or cry together like we used to do. Lord Jesus, let us get back to way it used to be. A family that prays together, not only stays together but get along better.

Amen!

1 Corinthians 13:4-7 New King James Version (NKJV)

"Love suffers long and is kind; love does not envy; love does not parade itself, is not [a]puffed up; 5 does not behave rudely, does not seek its own, is not provoked, [b]thinks no evil; 6 does not rejoice in iniquity, but rejoices in the truth; 7 bears all things, believes all things, hopes all things, endures all things".

1 Corinthians 13:4-7 The Message (MSG)

"If I give everything I own to the poor and even go to the stake to be burned as a martyr, but I don't love, I've gotten nowhere. So, no matter what I say, what I believe, and what I do, I'm bankrupt without love.

Love never gives up.
Love cares more for others than for self.
Love doesn't want what it doesn't have.
Love doesn't strut,
Doesn't have a swelled head,
Doesn't force itself on others,
Isn't always "me first,"
Doesn't fly off the handle,
Doesn't keep score of the sins of others,
Doesn't revel when others grovel,
Takes pleasure in the flowering of truth,
Puts up with anything,
Trusts God always,
Always looks for the best,
Never looks back,
But keeps going to the end.

Back in Da' Day, we set the table and blessed the food. No elbows on the table and we sat up straight. The new generation couldn't have made it back then. There were no cell phones glued to our ears.

LOL! This is what it was like every Sunday evening at dinner. Mama, auntie and all the kids came together, sat at the table to eat and enjoyed each other. It was our togetherness and laughter that made dinner so good, not just the taste of the food. These were some of the best days of my life.

LOVE

Father God,

Don't let parents be scared of their children. Lord, show parents how to control their homes and their children. Help parents learn how to discipline the child without abusing them. Lord, help parents love their children even when they are disciplining them. There is nothing wrong with discipline, God disciplines His children. Stand up and be the parent, not their best friend. Then, they will love you in the end for setting a good, Godly example.

Amen!

Proverbs 12:1 New King James Version (NKJV)

"Whoever loves instruction loves knowledge, but he who hates correction is stupid."

Proverbs 12:1 The Message (MSG)

"If you love learning, you love the discipline that goes with it— how shortsighted to refuse correction!"

Back in Da' Day, we got spankings with a switch. We even had to go outside and pick the switch off of the tree. And if you got the wrong size (on purpose), you marched right back out the door and got another one the right size that time. Now days, if this happened, the parents would have a case of child abuse. We survived the whippings, but look at us now. We still have all of our limbs and mama and daddy didn't go to jail. LOL!

DISCIPLINE

Jesus,

Let the children of this generation know what it is to help around the house. Encourage their hearts to pick up a broom or mop, wash dishes and vacuum floors. Lord, give them the initiative to want to help out with the household chores. Let them take pride in the upkeep of their homes.

Lord Jesus, help us teach them how to help their mothers or fathers in their home. Show them that there is more to life than playstation and cellphones. Don't let them be stuck inside watching social feeds and television all day long. Jesus, please show them the beauty of life, the value of life that you so freely give to each of us. Let the children want more out of life, a career, a family, or even a business of their own. Lord, let them grow up with a desire to be something greater as you have given them various skills and talents. Let them grow up to be somebody of importance, of value in their community and in the world. Lord let them grow up in your presence. Let them live a Godly life. Lord, show them the way.

Amen!

Colossians 3:23 New King James Version (NKJV)

"And whatever you do, do it heartily, as to the Lord and not to men."

Colossians 3:23-25 The Message (MSG)

"Servants, do what you're told by your earthly masters. And don't just do the minimum that will get you by. Do your best. Work from the heart for your real Master, for God, confident that you'll get paid in full when you come into your inheritance. Keep in mind always that the ultimate Master you're serving is Christ. The sullen servant who does shoddy work will be held responsible. Being a follower of Jesus doesn't cover up bad work."

Back in Da' Day, moma would say, if you are bored, I will give you something to do. Mop the floor, clean the dishes, and take out the trash. And when you get bored again, I have more for you to do. Please do not use the word bored again in life. I stopped telling my mother I was bored.

LEADER

God,

Now days everyone wants to be a leader. But no one wants to follow the wrong leader. We know that there is only one leader, Our Lord, Jesus Christ. Let us know your Holy Word so that we don't get caught up with the wrong teachings, following the wrong leaders. People will tell you what you want to hear. They will make it sound good to you, especially if you don't know the Word of God for yourself. In this world, it seems like right is wrong and wrong is right. God, lead us and guide us. God be with us. God teach us right from wrong.

Amen!

1 Timothy 4:12 King James Version (NKJV)
"Let no man despise thy youth; but be thou an example of the believers, in word, in conversation, in charity, in spirit, in faith, in purity."

1 Timothy 4:12-14 The Message Bible (MSG)

"Get the word out. Teach all these things. And don't let anyone put you down because you're young. Teach believers with your life: by word, by demeanor, by love, by faith, by integrity. Stay at your post reading Scripture, giving counsel, teaching."

Back in Da' Day, as kids we had a lot of fun joking around with each other. My cousin, Mack Earl (deceased), was our leader. He had us doing so many things that was not right, but fun to us. We did things and suffered the consequences later. One Sunday, we were all at the dinner table and Mack was told to bless the food. All of a sudden he belted out this verse that we knew was just not right, but we laughed anyway. He said, 'Jesus wept, and Moses crept where all the women slept.' We laughed so hard, but we knew we were in trouble. So, we all suffered the consequences because we followed our leader. The leader who got us all in trouble. Mama blessed the table from then on.

FORGIVENESS

Dear God,

My mother would encourage us to forgive people that hurt you and not hold grudges. She would let us know that when you don't forgive and hold grudges, you give them power over you. You would never be able to move forward. Our prayer should be just like the Lord's Prayer, *"forgive me as I forgive those that trespass against me."* Lord, don't let me hold a grudge against people. Let me move on in love because he have loved us. Despite all of the bad things that we do as people and do to other people, He love us anyway. So, show me how to love like you Lord. Show me how to live in peace with that person who has hurt me. Show me how to smile when I'm around them and not feel ill-will in my heart about them. Sometimes we have to laugh to keep from crying. Lord Jesus, give me my power back.

Amen!

Romans 12:14-21 New King James Version (NKJV)

"Bless those who persecute you; bless and do not curse. Rejoice with those who rejoice, and weep with those who weep. Be of the same mind toward one another. Do not set your mind on high things, but associate with the humble. Do not be wise in your own opinion.

Repay no one evil for evil. Have[a] regard for good things in the sight of all men. If it is possible, as much as depends on you, live peaceably with all men. Beloved, do not avenge yourselves, but rather give place to wrath; for it is written, "Vengeance is Mine, I will repay," says the Lord.

Therefore, "If your enemy is hungry, feed him; If he is thirsty, give him a drink; For in so doing you will heap coals of fire on his head." Do not be overcome by evil, but overcome evil with good."

Romans 12:14-21 The Message Bible (MSG)

"Bless your enemies; no cursing under your breath. Laugh with your happy friends when they're happy; share tears when they're down. Get along with each other; don't be stuck-up. Make friends with nobodies; don't be the great somebody.

Don't hit back; discover beauty in everyone. If you've got it in you, get along with everybody. Don't insist on getting even; that's not for you to do. "I'll do the judging," says God. "I'll take care of it."

Our Scriptures tell us that if you see your enemy hungry, go buy that person lunch, or if he's thirsty, get him a drink. Your generosity will surprise him with goodness. Don't let evil get the best of you; get the best of evil by doing good."

Back in Da' Day, My mother said something that sounded harsh, but truthful. For the person that hurt you, you don't have to be their friend. Forgive them and move on. Feed them with a long handled spoon. She meant, that you can be nice and treat them nice, but you don't have to be their friend. She said let God fight that battle for you. Mama meant what she said and said what she meant. I have seen her in action. She was just keeping it real. There are some people you just have to love them from afar.

OBEDIENCE

Jesus,

Let us keep our families close to us. Don't let us give in to letting the kids stay out late, not knowing where they are or who they are with. There is so much evil in this world we live in. People are not true to who they are. And they're not true to you either. Father God, let us not block our family from having fun, but help us to know that fun ends and we're home at a decent hour.

Amen!

Deuteronomy 11:27-28 King James Version (KJV)

"*A blessing, if ye obey the commandments of the* LORD *your God, which I command you this day: And a curse, if ye will not obey the commandments of the* LORD *your God, but turn aside out of the way which I command you this day, to go after other gods, which ye have not known."*

Deuteronomy 11:27-30 The Message (MSG)

"The Blessing: if you listen obediently to the commandments of GOD, your God, which I command you today. The Curse: if you don't pay attention to the commandments of GOD, your God, but leave the road that I command you today, following other gods of which you know nothing."

Back in Da' Day, mama said, "You'd better be in front of this house by the time the street lights come on. Not across the street, down the street, or around the corner. I mean inside this house." Oh well, there went my fun.

KINDNESS

Father God Almighty,

Touch our hearts and minds to take away the cold hearted feelings we have for people. This is for girls, boys, men and women. It is not okay to bully. Bullying is very hurtful, harmful, and evil. It's not okay to hurt people. We hurt people in so many ways, - with our actions, our ways, and certainly with our tongues. We don't value people and families don't appreciate one another. We don't pick up the phone to say hello or to just talk anymore like we used to do. What happened to us, Lord Jesus? The kids are mean to other kids and so on. We are the people of God. Big, little, young and old are all made in the image of God. So why we tripping off, black, white, red, or blue skin color? Now, I hope not red or blue skin, lol. The truth is, if you cut any of us we all bleed the same color. People must stop thinking that you're better than the next person. You may have a little more, but guess what, when you leave this earth, you can't take anything with you. So straighten up and fly right. Lord Jesus, show us the way and touch our hearts, In the Name of Jesus. Amen.

Mark 12:30-31 New King James Version (NKJV)

"And you shall love the Lord your God with all your heart, with all your soul, with all your mind, and with all your strength. 'This is the first commandment. And the second, like it, is this: 'You shall love your neighbor as yourself.' There is no other commandment greater than these."

Mark 12:30-31 The Message Bible (MSG)

"Jesus said, "The first in importance is, 'Listen, Israel: The Lord your God is one; so love the Lord God with all your passion and prayer and intelligence and energy.' And here is the second: 'Love others as well as you love yourself.' There is no other commandment that ranks with these."

Back in Da' Day, my mother would hear me being mean to one of my friends and she would say, "If that is your friend, you don't treat them like that. And the same goes for your family members." She would reward me with 50 cents for all the friends I treated nice. OMG! Back then, that was a lot of money for us to buy a lot of junk food and candy. But I look at that now and think, what can I do with that now? I can't buy gum or candy out of the machine with 50 cents. The kids nowadays would think we were crazy if we said we will give a 50 cents.

I used to catch the bus years ago to my job downtown and I remember waiting on the bus stop one day. A young guy came up to me and asked me for $2. He had the nerve to tell me that it was hard out here and he doesn't want to work or have any responsibility. So, he chose to live on the streets. But me being me, I had to have the last word. I said, "But you are out here begging me for my hard earned money? I get up early and go to work, regardless of the rain, snow, sleet, or hail. And you have the nerve to ask me for $2, not just $1 but $2. No, I don't think so." He walked off and said, I knew you wouldn't give me nothing. Then, he called me out of my name. I, then had a flashback, and I thought about that childhood phrase - Sticks and stones may break my bones, but words will never hurt me. By this time I'm all riled up because he was trying me, but it didn't work. Next thing I know, he was asking the next guy waiting on the bus stop for $5. I couldn't believe it. Some people are just like that, but hey, you don't have to be like that.

HEALING

Lord Jesus,

Please heal my body! Touch, heal, and deliver us from all the sickness and pain that is taking over our bodies. Remove any diseases or infirmity that shouldn't be there. Lord, remove diabetes, cancer, arthritis, and migraines. Lord, make my body new. I ask you to remove the need for daily medications to live and function. Lord, we trust you as our medicine. You are the Great Physician, we depend on you to take care of us.

Amen!

Jeremiah 17:14 New King James Version (NKJV)

"Heal me, O LORD, and I shall be healed; Save me, and I shall be saved, for You are my praise.

Jeremiah 17:14-18 the Message Bible (MSG)

"GOD, pick up the pieces. Put me back together again. You are my praise!"

Back in Da' Day, I remember hearing the older people say, "I can tell it is going to rain, snow, sleet, hail because of the aches and pains in my body. Old Arthur (Arthritis) is visiting me today". Now, I know exactly what they were talking about. I'm a living witness.

GOD FEARING

God,

Will you show our younger generations how to respect their elders? God, grant them integrity, value, and character as young people to honor those who have come before them. Children can be so disrespectful nowadays. They will walk by you and not speak. They won't open their mouths. They walk in front of you, but not hold the door open for you. Teach them Lord! And encourage their parents to teach them as well. They want to have the last word. Lord, show them when and how to keep their mouths shut and just listen. Help them not to talk back, but to have and show respect when they're being spoken to by the elderly.

Amen!

Leviticus 19:32 New King James Version (NKJV)

"You shall [a]rise before the gray headed and honor the presence of an old man, and fear your God: I am the LORD."

Leviticus 19:32 The Message Bible (MSG)

"Show respect to the aged; honor the presence of an elder; fear your God. I am GOD."

Back in Da' Day, I remember my mother talking and fussing at me. I kept on talking and not listening. My mother shouted at me, one lying, tell the other to hush. I recall telling her to hush. The next thing I remember is her hand across my lips. That was the last time that I tried telling to hush. Now days we have special lipsticks to make your lips plump, but my mother was the manufacture of plump lips back in the day. LOL!

SACRIFICE

God,

Please keep us obedient to Your Word. Keep us walking on that straight and narrow path called righteousness. God, I know you know that it get hard for us sometimes and we fall off the wagon. We go on our own paths which lead to destruction. I ask you, Lord Jesus, to keep us especially when we have trouble keeping ourself. You said in your word that *"Obedience is better than sacrifice",* so I am crying out to you Lord to be obedient and I thank you for your help in doing so.

Amen!

Isaiah 1:19 New King James Version (NKJV)

"If you are willing and obedient, You shall eat the good of the land;"

Isaiah 1:19-20 The Message Bible (MSG)

"Come. Sit down. Let's argue this out."
This is God's Message:
"If your sins are blood-red,
they'll be snow-white.
If they're red like crimson,
they'll be like wool.
If you'll willingly obey,
you'll feast like kings.
But if you're willful and stubborn,
you'll die like dogs."
That's right. God says so."

Back in Da' Day, and even now, I can hear in the back of my mind when I am not falling out of obedience. "How many times does the Lord have to knock you upside your head before you get it right?" I've taken so many hard knocks upside my head, have you? I think that's where some of those headaches came from. OMG!

GRACE

God,

Please watch over me! Guide my footsteps. Give me grace to face whatever may come my way. Guide me with your eye and keeping me from making the same mistakes I made in the past. God, let your eye follow me, lead me, teach me, walk with me, and talk with me. Thank you for your mercy that are new every morning. Your grace and mercy just keeps on keeping me.

Amen!

2 Corinthians 12:9 King James Version (KJV)

"And he said unto me, my grace is sufficient for thee: for my strength is made perfect in weakness. Most gladly therefore will I rather glory in my infirmities, that the power of Christ may rest upon me."

2 Corinthians 12:9 The Message Bible (MSG) (MSG)

"My grace is enough; it's all you need. My strength comes into its own in your weakness."

Back in Da' Day, moma knew when you done something wrong. Her saying was, "Didn't you know I had eyes in the back of my head?" I couldn't get by with doing wrong then and I still can't today. God is watching you with His righteous eye.

ANGER

Dear God,

Please help me to keep my mouth from quarreling with people. Help me to control my anger. Let me withdraw from the conversation when it causes anger or frustration to rise up in me. There are times when people will take you to an angry place and make you go there. Lord, show me how to restrain myself from all foolishness that comes from arguing with people. I know there are some that will not stop until they have the last word. Lord Jesus, help me keep my mouth shut from saying the wrong thing. Help me put my mouth on mute and only unmute when you know it's safe for me to speak without displeasing you with my words.

Amen!

Proverbs 26:4-5 New King James Version (NKJV)

"*Do not answer a fool according to his folly, Lest you also be like him. Answer a fool according to his folly, Lest he be wise in his own eyes.*"

Proverbs 26:4-5 The Message Bible (MSG)

"*Don't respond to the stupidity of a fool; you'll only look foolish yourself. Answer a fool in simple terms so he doesn't get a swelled head.*"

Back in Da' Day, moma would always say, "Let the fool have the last word". I found out that a fool will continue to argue until the cows come home. Another one of mama's sayings of wisdom from the heart.

CHILDREN OF GOD

God.

I remember as a kid during the holidays, we had Church programs. We had an Easter program, a Fall program and a Christmas program. All of the children had a speech to learn and read during the program. God, can we or will we get back to those days again? It was so nice to see and hear children speaking to God. The girls would dress up in little dresses and patent leather shoes while the boys would wear a suit and tie. I really missed those days!

Matthew 19:14-15 New King James Version (NKJV)

"But Jesus said, "Let the little children come to Me, and do not forbid them; for of such is the kingdom of heaven." And He laid His hands on them and departed from there."

Matthew 19:14-15 The Message (MSG)

"One day children were brought to Jesus in the hope that he would lay hands on them and pray over them. The disciples shooed them off. But Jesus intervened: "Let the children alone, don't prevent them from coming to me. God's kingdom is made up of people like these." After laying hands on them, he left."

Back in Da' Day, my mother would be so mad at me. She would dress me up for the program. She would take the time to help me learn the speech, and guess what? Being my shy self, I would get up to say my speech and all of a sudden start crying. I can see my moma's face right now. My niece would run up to the microphone and say loudly, "Come on, I'll say your speech with you." Moma was furious, but so glad that I was off the stage. My moma stayed mad at me for a little while for that. LOL

LOVE, SMILE AND BE KIND

Lord Jesus,

We need you today like never before. Our world is in bad shape. We do not value anything, people, places, or things. Lord Jesus, show us how to love. Show us how to treat people. Lord Jesus just show us the way we're supposed to be. We are made in your image and likeness, but what happened to us? Why do we hurt the people we love, then try to love the people we hurt? You love us unconditionally, so why can't we do the same? I'm crying out to you Lord Jesus. Thank you for loving us. Amen.

Matthew 7:13-14 New King James Version (NKJV)

"Enter by the narrow gate; for wide is the gate and broad is the way that leads to destruction, and there are many who go in by it. Because narrow is the

gate and [b]difficult is the way which leads to life, and there are few who find it."

Matthew 7:13-14 The Message Bible (MSG)

"Don't look for shortcuts to God. The market is flooded with surefire, easygoing formulas for a successful life that can be practiced in your spare time. Don't fall for that stuff, even though crowds of people do. The way to life—to God!—is vigorous and requires total attention."

Back in Da' Day, remember sticks and stones may break my bones, but words will never hurt me. We know that is true, words truly hurt and words never leave you. When we were young, we believed this. But now we know, words have an everlasting effect on people. Use your words wisely. Never burn bridges because you never know when you have to cross that bridge again, and always treat people the way you want to be treated.

HONOR

Dear God!

Thank you for this day! Thank you for my family! But God let them act right today! Let my children do what they are told to do today. Don't let their mouths fly off the handle. Let them abide by the rules of this house today. Keep them Lord Jesus. Keep your arm of protection around them forever!

Amen!

Ephesians 6:1-4 King James Version (KJV)

"Children, obey your parents in the Lord: for this is right. Honour thy father and mother; which is the first commandment with promise; That it may be well with thee, and thou mayest live long on the earth. And, ye fathers, provoke not your children to wrath: but bring them up in the nurture and admonition of the Lord."

Ephesians 6:1-4 The Message (MSG)

Children, do what your parents tell you. This is only right. "Honor your father and mother" is the first commandment that has a promise attached to it, namely, "so you will live well and have a long life. Fathers, don't exasperate your children by coming down hard on them. Take them by the hand and lead them in the way of the Master.

Back in Da' Day, and still today it's good for children to listen to their parents. Still to this day I remember the saying, "Keep talking and I will slap you into next week." You remember that? LOL!

TRUST

Lord Jesus,

We need you so badly in this day and age. Where has the trust gone? In this world, a title means nothing. The trust level is at an all low for authority figures, leaders and those who govern over others. We think we know people, but when you turn around the trust is gone. God, I know you are trying to show us to put our trust in only you. We all are in need of your grace and mercy. Will you send it Lord? Help us!

Amen!

Psalm 118:8 New King James Version (NKJV)

"It is better to trust in the LORD Than to put confidence in man."

Psalm 118:8 The Message Bible (MSG)

"Far better to take refuge in GOD than trust in people; Far better to take refuge in GOD than trust in celebrities."

Back in Da' Day, I remember my mother telling me "Do not put your trust in everyone." People will fail you. Put your trust in God. He never fails, give up on you, or will never leave you.

DESTRUCTION

Dear Lord,

We often make bad decisions. Bad choices. Bad everything, from time to time. We don't listen to the people that love us and tell us we are headed in the wrong direction. Instead, we do things our own way which is a type of 'bad' choice. God has given us free will which is when we choose. More often than not, we neglect God's will or way, but go with our own will and way, which leads to destruction every time. Lord, give us the strength to stop being stupid. Will you show us how to 'move off of stupid' meaning get our head out of the clouds and start paying attention to what's really going on in life. Lord, this sounds harsh, but it is the truth. I have been there so many times. I thank you Lord for opening my eyes to see my mistakes and to turn to you for guidance and direction in my life.

Amen!

Deuteronomy 28:1-2, 15-20 New King James Version (NKJV)

"Now it shall come to pass, if you diligently obey the voice of the LORD your God, to observe carefully all His commandments which I command you today, and that the LORD your God will set you high above all nations of the earth. And all these blessings shall come upon you and overtake you, because you obey the voice of the LORD your God: Curses on Disobedience. *"*

"But it shall come to pass, if you do not obey the voice of the LORD your God, to observe carefully all His commandments and His statutes which I command you today, that all these curses will come upon you and overtake you: 'Cursed shall you be in the city, and cursed shall you be in the country. "Cursed shall be your basket and your kneading bowl. "Cursed shall be the fruit of your body and the produce of your land, the increase of your cattle and the offspring of your flocks. "Cursed shall you be when you come in, and cursed shall you be when you go out. "The LORD will send on you cursing, confusion, and rebuke in all that you set your hand to do, until you are destroyed and until you perish quickly, because of the wickedness of your doings in which you have forsaken Me.

Deuteronomy 28:1-2; 15-20 The Message Bible (MSG)

If you listen obediently to the Voice of GOD, your God, and heartily obey all his commandments that I command you today, GOD, your God, will place you on high, high above all the nations of the world. All these blessings will come down on you and spread out beyond you because you have responded to the Voice of GOD, your God:

Here's what will happen if you don't obediently listen to the Voice of GOD, your God, and diligently keep all the commandments and guidelines that I'm commanding you today. All these curses will come down hard on you:

GOD's curse in the city,
GOD's curse in the country;
GOD's curse on your basket and bread bowl;
GOD's curse on your children,
the crops of your land,
the young of your livestock,
the calves of your herds,
the lambs of your flocks.
GOD's curse in your coming in,
GOD's curse in your going out.

GOD will send The Curse, The Confusion, The Contrariness down on everything you try to do until you've been destroyed and there's nothing left of you—all because of your evil pursuits that led you to abandon me."

Back in Da' Day, I remember my mother telling me this so many times, "A hard head makes a soft behind". What she meant by that was if you didn't have the sense to stop making bad choices. You'd fall on that butt enough times, it gets softer and softer with every bad decision. Eventually, you'd come to your senses and stop causing yourself to fall so often.

WORSHIP

Jesus,

Protect us as we come and as we go. Lord, guide us to your house of worship and praise. Let us come into your house with thanksgiving and into your courts with praise. Let us come with a grateful heart, with praise and worship on our hearts and lips. Let us come because we desire to be with you and not like we're going to work. Lord, let this be something that we want to do and not because some is making us come.

Amen!

Hebrews 10:25 New King James Version (NKJV)

"Not forsaking the assembling of ourselves together, as is the manner of some, but exhorting one another, and so much the more as you see the Day approaching."

Hebrews 10:25 The Message (MSG)

"So let's do it—full of belief, confident that we're presentable inside and out. Let's keep a firm grip on the promises that keep us going. He always keeps his word. Let's see how inventive we can be in encouraging love and helping out, not avoiding worshiping together as some do but spurring each other on, especially as we see the big Day approaching."

Back in Da' Day, if we didn't get up to go to church, we'd be in the house for the next four weekends. My mama didn't play when it came to church. We went to Sunday school, regular service, and sometimes an evening service at the church. If you complained and said you wasn't feeling well and stayed home (with her permission). You stayed home from playing and hanging out with your friends for the next month also. Now I can't stay away from the church house. I was glad when they said unto me, 'Let us go into the house of the Lord'.

HOLY

Father God,

I pray for our teenage girls and boys. They need your guidance in everything that they do. Watch over them everywhere they go and show them the way. Lord, show them how to present themselves to the world. Help them know that the world is twisted and sinful. Lord, help them know the difference between. Lord Jesus, show our teen girl how to dress modestly. Let them see themselves like you see them, so that they're lovely when they go out and not unkempt. We know that this is not what you had in mind for them. Lord Jesus, show the teen boys that pants are to be pulled up and stayed on their waist with a belt. It's not a good look dragging and sagging around the knees. No one should be able to see their underwear. If they don't have anyone to show them how to keep themselves looking honorable, provide a 'ram in the bush'.

Bring someone into their lives to guide, direct and protect them as they venture out in the world. Teenagers always present yourselves to the world as neat and professional, not any kind of way. Do not give away your self-worth. Even if you are not accepted by some, you are definitely accepted by Jesus Christ. You are made in the image of Christ, so please represent Him well.

Amen!

Romans 12:1 New King James Version (NKJV)

"I beseech you therefore, brethren, by the mercies of God, that you present your bodies a living sacrifice, holy, acceptable to God, which is your reasonable service."

Romans 12:1-2 The Message Bible (MSG)

"So here's what I want you to do, God helping you: Take your everyday, ordinary life—your sleeping, eating, going-to-work, and walking-around life— and place it before God as an offering. Embracing what God does for you is the best thing you can do for him. Don't become so well-adjusted to your culture that you fit into it without even thinking. Instead, fix your attention on God. You'll be changed from the

inside out. Readily recognize what he wants from you, and quickly respond to it. Unlike the culture around you, always dragging you down to its level of immaturity, God brings the best out of you, develops well-formed maturity in you."

Back in Da' Day, and I think it's still true now. Boys don't want fast tail girls. Likewise, girls don't want trifling boys. These words were engraved in my head and heart. Your mothers and fathers only want what is best for you. No offense.

A FINAL WORD FROM
THE AUTHOR

I started writing this book in the summer of 2019. I had no idea that it would come to a complete stop with me getting sick and living through the COVID-19 pandemic.All of a sudden my life changed seemed like. I started working from home in March 2020 and the saga began. At the beginning of my illness, I was diagnosed with bronchitis which turned into an upper respiratory infection. I was given a CT scan of my lungs which showed that I had enlarged lymph nodes. Next, came the sinus infection. My first time in the ER, I was given a COVID test, which came back negative. The doctor looked at me and said, "You are sick". The second time in the ER, I couldn't breathe and just felt sick. I was given another COVID blood test, which came back negative. I was on so much medication that it made me cough continuously, lose weight, and made my hair shed. I got hives and the list goes on.

Now, the third trip to the ER was by ambulance. My husband didn't know what to do because once again, I couldn't breathe. The paramedic said that my chest was so tight and that I was sick. In the ambulance, they gave me oxygen to help me breathe. Then, another round of medicine and again I heard, "You are really sick". There were nights it was so bad that I was afraid to go to sleep. I wasn't sure if I would wake up the next morning. I had Twayne to pray and watch over me as I slept. I tried to sleep sitting up. I would walk the halls until early morning praying and asking God to heal my body. I'd say, please keep me God, so I can see and be with my family. I didn't share all my bouts with this sickness with my family because I didn't want them to worry. I thank my family for praying for me. My prayer for myself was Psalm 91. I would pray that prayer, night and day - day and night.

At the end of July I had sinus surgery, it had gotten that bad. At first, that was very difficult and I was a little nervous. But it worked and helped me. I had so many inhalers that the doctors had given me. I lost my voice. My voice was very hoarse and my throat would hurt. I then had to go in for a biopsy on my thyroid due to a nodule. After sending the results back and forth to specialist, I thanked God it was not cancerous. It was a very scary time in my life. I really tried not to worry. I kept saying to myself, "If I am praying I shouldn't worry and if I am worrying myself about it, then I shouldn't be praying". I knew that God is a healer and that He was in control of my sickness. The doctors were very concerned about the hoarseness in my throat. Come to find out, I had a yeast infection on my vocal cords caused by the use of all the inhalers. OMG! What else will I have to face or overcome?

As of now, I am much better. I feel so much better. It turns out that I have Eosinophil Asthma. This is the first time I've ever had asthma. I have moved from inhalers to injections which really help me. Initially, I was terrified when I learned about taking the injections because of possible side effects. This medicine, that I now have to inject monthly, has a $1000mo copay. I praise God for my doctor, because without them, I wouldn't have known where to start for co-pay reduction. But God! I now have to carry an Epinephrine pen with me at all times. My life has changed and I thank God for bringing me through.

We never know what God has in store for us. We have plans to do things our way, but God intervenes and take us on a different path. We don't always understand it, but as long as God is leading the way, we know it'll be alright. We have to keep striving ahead. I remember my girlfriend teaching a bible study class and saying, "You have to do it afraid". There is a fear of the unknown that we all experience from time to time. There were days for me that I didn't think I would pull through, but God! God had my hand and was leading me. The Lord led me to write this portion about my illness. It's to let people know that they can make it as long as you have God on your side, in your heart, your soul, and your spirit.

In the midst of getting better, I was called into a meeting with my manager. She told me that my position was eliminated and that I would be laid off. My last day with the company was going to be on March 4th which was only a few weeks away. I handled it well. I wanted God to be pleased with me so I took the news very well. But I had to ask God the question, "What is going on with me? What is next for me?" I knew without a shadow of a doubt that God had much more for me to do. So, I just kept on striving and doing my best.

I just want to encourage every reader - keep God close and see what He makes happen for you. We are all in the palm of His hand and He knows what the future holds for all of us. Even when we don't know, He does. Thank you God!

I want to thank my husband Twayne for taking care of me when I couldn't care for myself. I want to thank my mother, whose face is on the cover. I felt her prayers all the way from Baltimore, MD. She called and checked on me daily. I love you mama. I want to thank my daughters for taking care of their mother. I love you ladies. And all my sisters, who also called and checked on me daily. My family prayed for me. To my friends who prayed for me. Many thanks to absolutely everyone! I love and appreciate you all.

I am the Author of "MY GOD! MY GOD!" This was my 1st book, which was published in 2007.

Brenda Hicks-Wiggins

www.ingramcontent.com/pod-product-compliance
Lightning Source LLC
Chambersburg PA
CBHW060643150426
42811CB00079B/2291/J